DUTCH CUISINE

COLOPHON

Food & recipes: Thea Spierings

Final editing: Marianne Top

Art direction & design: Suzanne Groenewegen

Photography: Jurriaan Huting, Remco Lassche,

Freek Stoltenborgh

Styling: Lize Boer

Assistant publisher: Josje Kets

Publisher Pieter Harts

English translation: Trahern Gemmell for Textcase,

Hilversum, Netherlands

With thanks to:

David Mulder, Lifestyle, Zus & Zo Keukengerei

© Visconti, 2008

1st printing 2008

© English edition: Miller Books

email: info@miller-books.com

www.miller-books.com

978 90 8724 084 4

INTRODUCTION

DUTCH CUISINE

Ever tried meal gruel, redcurrant delight or homemade fried fillets of haddock? And when was the last time you prepared red cabbage with apples from scratch, or meat stew? (Re)discover traditional Dutch cuisine with Deliciously Dutch, and at the same time find out how to update these classical dishes using the new and exciting makeovers in this book.

For centuries Dutch cooking followed the rhythm of the seasons. People ate what was locally grown, the emphasis being on sustenance. Accordingly, daily food was whatever was available. Plentiful fresh produce in spring and summer, lots of earthy, heart warming dishes in autumn and rich, heavy fare in winter. This did not necessarily add up to what would nowadays be considered a healthy diet. However, it was a cuisine that brought with it a longing for the next season's delicacies. The first spring greens, sweet summertime strawberries or succulent autumn game. It was about eating the right food at the right moment.

Times have changed but many Dutch dishes are as delicious as ever. And because freshly prepared food, using fresh seasonal ingredients will always taste the best, this book is divided into seasonal sections. Each of the four chapters provides recipes for two soups, a starter or side dish, six main dishes and two desserts. Accompanying these are great culinary ideas and recipes for dazzling new versions of old favourites, updates that transform them into exciting, healthy and modern dishes, perfectly suiting the fusion-cooking style of Holland today.

Each season concludes with a wonderful three course menu - often exploring international influences - illustrating how to make the most of the available seasonal produce. These dishes take their inspiration from the best traditions of Dutch cuisine: pure and honest, easy-to-prepare food which uses widely available ingredients, always stylishly presented.

A new Dutch culinary adventure starts right here, with Dutch Cuisine.

Note: all recipes serve 4 people unless otherwise stated.

TABLE OF CONTENTS

SPRING

MARCH - APRIL - MAY

VEGETABLE SOUP
WITH MEATBALLS

500g (17.6oz) soup greens

1 small bunch parsley, finely chopped

5 sprigs of celery, finely chopped

1½ l (51floz) beef stock

200g (7oz) minced beef (US ground beef)

75g (2.6oz) vermicelli

salt and pepper

1   Bring the soup greens, parsley, celery, and beef stock to the boil. Simmer gently for 5 minutes on a low heat.

2   Meanwhile, season the mince (ground beef) with salt and pepper and form small meat balls for the soup.

3   Stir the meatballs and the vermicelli into the soup and cook for 5 minutes till done.

An alternative recipe:

Give your soup a Mediterranean twist by adding a spoonful of pesto to each plate just before serving. This Italian delicacy is made from olive oil, garlic, basil leaves, Pecorino or Parmesan cheese and pine nuts and has been a popular tapenade in the Netherlands for years.

PURSLANE SOUP

150g (5.3oz) minced beef (ground beef)

1l (33.8floz) vegetable stock

500g (17.6oz) purslane, cut finely

1 tbsp olive oil

2 onions, finely chopped

1 leek, sliced into thin rings

1 tbsp coarse mustard

pepper and salt

1   Mix the mince (ground beef) together with a little pepper and salt and form into little soup balls.

2   Bring the stock to the boil, add the purslane to the stock and let it reduce. Next, purée the soup with a hand-mixer.

3   Heat the oil in a frying pan and fry the onions and leek. Add the mustard to this mixture and mix it into the soup.

4   Stir the soup balls into the soup and allow it to simmer gently until well-cooked.

5   If necessary add some extra pepper and salt.

An alternative recipe:

Cows in the meadows, lambs being born, fruit trees in bloom: it's spring again. At the end of April, the first leafy vegetables will be harvested from the fields: spinach, turnip tops, lamb's lettuce, and wonderfully fresh purslane. Purslane has a clean crisp taste that is really appropriate to the spring season. The soup will gain more punch if you use 200g (7oz) Gorgonzola instead of the meat balls. Pop this in at the last minute and let it melt. Do not purée with a hand blender! Garnish with a little Parmesan.

RUSSIAN SALAD

250g (8.8oz) meat for soup,
cooked and diced

2 sour apples, peeled and cubed

8 potatoes, cooked,
cooled and diced

6 small gherkins (pickles), cubed

10 silver onions, cubed

2 tbsp olive oil

1 tsp vinegar

1 tsp mustard

1 tbsp sugar

2 tbsp mayonnaise

pepper and salt

1   Mix the meat, potatoes, gherkins and silver onions and toss with
    a little oil, vinegar, mustard and sugar. Stir in the mayonnaise.
2   Season with pepper and salt.
3   Serve in a large dish and garnish with slices of gherkin.

100g (3.5oz) green peas
a little basil, finely chopped
2 tomatoes, seeded and diced
1 red onion in half rings
2 tbsp pine nuts, roasted

An alternative recipe:

This traditional Russian salad is omnipresent at almost
every birthday. It is often served on a large, flat dish and
garnished with lettuce, cucumber, tomato and gherkin.
Why not make your salad a bit more festive? Add the
ingredients opposite to the existing recipe and leave out
the mayonnaise. The dressing with vinegar and olive oil is
fine on its own.

TURNIP TOP HOTCHPOTCH

WITH FRESH SAUSAGE

1kg (35.3oz) potatoes,

cooked and cut into pieces.

small knob of butter

dash of milk

nutmeg

4 sausages

500g (17.6oz) turnip tops, washed,

roots removed and cut

into small pieces

salt

1   Heat the butter and fry the sausages till nice and brown.

2   Mash the potatoes, butter and milk together.

3   Season the mash with a little salt and nutmeg.

4   Stir in the turnip tops just before dishing up and serve with
    the sausages.

An alternative recipe:

Turnip tops are truly Dutch vegetables from the olden days. This vegetable has a strong taste, is rich in minerals and contains a lot of iron and lots of vitamins. You can make this a vegetarian dish by using 200g (7oz) of Gorgonzola. Stir this carefully into the hotchpotch at the very last minute. Make sure the hotchpotch is really warm.

SPINACH
WITH SMALL POTATOES

500g (17.6oz) spinach, washed

1kg (35.3oz) small potatoes,
in their jackets

25g 0.88oz) butter

4 hard boiled eggs

pinch of nutmeg

small amount of parsley,
finely chopped

pepper and salt

1   Put the spinach in a large pan with a little boiling water.

2   Cook the spinach on low heat for about 5 minutes until it is soft,
keep the lid on the pan.

3   Heat the butter in the pan and fry the potatoes for about ten
minutes till cooked.

4   Strain the spinach in a colander. Try to drain off as much water
as possible. If necessary, drain off more water by using a saucer to
press it out.

5   Cut the spinach finely and stir in the butter and nutmeg.
Season with salt and pepper.

6   Portion the potatoes and spinach onto 4 plates and garnish the
spinach with egg.

An alternative recipe:

The Netherlands are well known for their variety of fresh
vegetables. Spinach is a delicious and healthy example.
Spinach does not always have to be prepared traditionally
but can also be stir-fried. Heat a little olive oil in a pan
and melt 6 anchovy fillets with a clove of (crushed) garlic.
Add the spinach, then take it out of the pan when
reduced.

WHITE ASPARAGUS
WITH HAM AND EGGS

2kg (70.5oz) white asparagus, peeled, woody ends cut off.
6 eggs, hard boiled, peeled and cut into pieces
100g (3.5oz) butter
½ lemon, squeezed
2-3 tbsp fresh parsley, finely chopped
nutmeg
200g (7oz) cooked ham, in slices
pepper and salt

1   Bring water to the boil in a large pan. Cook the asparagus in the boiling water for 10 minutes. Take the pan off the heat and leave the asparagus in the water for another 10 minutes. Strain the asparagus in a colander.

2   Push the eggs through a sieve using the round side of a spoon.

3   Melt the butter in a pan and mix in the lemon juice. Season with a little salt and pepper.

4   Put the asparagus next to each other in a dish, with the heads in the same direction and pour some of the butter sauce over them. Sprinkle the egg crumbs and parsley over the dish. Flavour with salt and pepper and nutmeg.

An alternative recipe:

There is no other vegetable that is so expectantly awaited as the Asparagus, the queen of vegetables. The Netherlands even have a Miss Asparagus Competition! This white gold is mostly produced in the Dutch provinces of Brabant and Limburg at the end of April. Give asparagus an Italian flavour by cutting it at an angle and then stir frying it for 5 minutes. At the last minute, add 200gr (7oz) Parma ham (cut into slivers) and 2 tablespoons (finely chopped) dried tomatoes in oil.

MACKEREL
WITH FRIED POTATOES AND SALAD

4 small mackerel, cleaned

4 eggs, hard boiled:

2 chopped finely and 2 in slices as garnish

100g (3.5oz) cheese, grated

1 tsp mustard

2 tbsp butter, melted

1 tbsp parsley, finely chopped

½ lemon, juice and grated peel

25g (0.88oz) butter

1kg (35.3oz) potatoes,

cooked and cut in slices

1 lettuce

1 Warm the oven to 180° Celsius (356° Fahrenheit), gas mark 4-5.

2 Make 3 cuts on both sides of the fish.

3 Mix the rest of the ingredients well and spread this mixture into grooves in the fish.

4 Grease a baking dish with butter, put the fish in the dish and cover them with aluminium foil.

5 Bake the mackerel for 40 minutes in a preheated oven till well-cooked.

6 Heat the butter in the frying pan and fry the potatoes till they are nice and brown.

7 Serve the mackerel with fried potatoes and lettuce garnished with slices of egg.

An alternative recipe:

Once, it was quite a job to preserve fatty fish such as mackerel. Fatty fish becomes rancid when exposed to air. Thanks to the invention of the fridge, this is no longer a problem. Pour 200ml (6.8floz) dry white wine into a baking dish. Add the mackerel fillet to the wine. Add 1 red pepper (seeded and in thin slices), 1 onion (diced) and 1cm (0.39inch) ginger (grated). Cook the fish at 180°C (356°Fahrenheit), gas mark 4-5 till ready.

PIKE FILLET
WITH PEAS AND CARROTS

4 pike fillets, about 120g (4.2oz) each

1 egg, beaten

breadcrumbs

2 tbsp butter

1 onion, diced

1 tbsp flour

100ml (3.4floz) stock

500g (17.6oz) peas and carrots, cooked

pepper and salt

1. Sprinkle the pike with salt and pepper.

2. Cook the carrots and peas in a pan with salted boiling water. Cook them for 10 minutes till they are ready but still firm.

3. Coat the fish on both sides with beaten egg and then coat with breadcrumbs till covered.

4. Heat 1 tablespoon butter in a pan and fry the pike golden brown. This takes about 5 minutes per side.

5. To make the onion dressing, melt the butter in a frying pan and fry the onion for 1 minute, add more butter and let it brown.

6. Pour the stock in the pan and add the flour, keep stirring till all the lumps have disappeared.

7. Portion the fillets onto 4 plates and serve with the carrots and peas. Serve the onion dressing separately.

An alternative recipe:

100ml (3.4floz) vegetable stock
100ml (3.4floz) dry white wine
1 leek finely chopped
2 tomatoes, in slices
100ml (3.4floz) cream
a sprinkling of finely chopped dill;
keep four sprigs for garnishing.

Pike also tastes great when oven-baked. Preheat the oven at 180°Celsius (356° Fahrenheit), gas mark 4-5. Bring the stock and the wine to the boil in a pan and then pour into an oven dish. Add the leek and the fish to the liquid and put in the oven for 8 minutes. Arrange the tomato on top and let it cook with the other ingredients for 2 minutes. Make sure the fish is done. Take the dish out of the oven and scoop the vegetables and fish out of the liquid and keep them warm. Sieve the liquid and pour it together with the cream into a pan, cook for three minutes, stir in the dill and cook for another minute. Purée with the hand blender.

FRIED FILLETS OF HADDOCK

4 haddock fillets, about 150g (5.3oz) each

1 tbsp lemon juice

2 eggs

100g (3.5oz) flour

2dl (6.76floz) milk

pan with oil for deep-frying

4 sprigs of parsley for garnishing

4 segments of lemon

pepper and salt

1   Heat the oil in a deep frying pan to 180° Celsius (356° Fahrenheit), gas mark 4-5.

2   Sprinkle the haddock with lemon juice and with a little salt and pepper.

3   Beat the eggs with salt and pepper and add the flour. Pour the milk in gradually. Keep stirring till the batter is smooth.

4   Coat the fish with the batter and then deep fry the fillets in the oil for about 6 minutes till they are golden brown and cooked. Drain them on kitchen paper.

5   Serve the haddock on a serving dish and garnish with parsley and lemon.

An alternative recipe:

Why not change the taste and the colour of the fish in a flash?
Add 4 tablespoons of red curry to the egg batter and there you have it!

SNOW PUDDING

1l (33.8floz) milk

½ vanilla pod

90g (3.2oz) sugar

100g (3.5) cornstarch

4 egg whites

1   Pour two thirds of the milk into a pan, then add the vanilla pod and let it simmer on low heat for a while.

2   Add sugar and bring to the boil.

3   Stir the rest of the milk and the cornstarch together till it becomes a thin gruel.

4   Take the vanilla pod out of the milk and pour the cornstarch gruel into the boiling milk while stirring constantly. Allow everything to cook till it becomes a thick mixture.

5   Whisk the egg whites till they are stiff, add the pudding and mix everything together well.

6   Grease 4 dessert dishes with a little egg white and pour the pudding into them. Put the pudding in the fridge and allow to cool for about 4 hours.

An alternative recipe:

It used to be important that the meal was nutritious and cheap. This is how snow pudding came into being, often prepared with eggs from people's own chickens. Nowadays we know that too many eggs are bad for cholesterol levels in our blood. However, three eggs a week is no problem. Add orange peel to the vanilla pod. Put 1 tablespoon of Grand Marnier in the milk and allow to simmer. Serve the pudding with segments of orange.

MEAL GRUEL

1l (33.8floz) milk
60g (2.1oz) flour
sugar
pinch of salt

1   Stir 50ml (1.7floz) of milk and flour together to make
    a creamy gruel.
2   Bring the rest of the milk and the salt to the boil. Stir in
    the gruel and allow to bind while stirring constantly.
3   Serve the meal gruel with sugar.

An alternative recipe:

Meal gruel was often eaten in the 19th and 20th centuries,
especially by little children. The recipe was sometimes
made with sweet milk as an added luxury. This simple
recipe can use a few extras. Enrich this dessert by cooking
lemon rind with the milk (remember to sieve it out again
before serving!). Stir in a tablespoon of honey at the last
moment and serve with 400g (14oz) fresh strawberries.
A truly Dutch dessert in a new guise; enjoy!

SPRING MENU

ASPARAGUS SALAD- RACK OF LAMB IN PANCETTA- LEMON MOUSSE

ASPARAGUS SALAD

WITH STRAWBERRIES AND PARMA HAM

500g (17.6oz) asparagus,

cooked, in pieces

mixed salad to the amount of ½ head

150g (5.3oz) strawberries, in halves

4 slices of Parma ham

For the strawberry dressing:

1 egg yolk

1 tsp mustard

2 tbsp vegetable stock

1 tsp strawberry or white wine vinegar

50g (1.8oz) strawberries

1 tsp honey

maize oil

1 Preheat the oven to 200°Celsius (392° Fahrenheit), gas mark 5-6.

2 Place the slices of ham in the oven and bake till crispy.

3 Mix all the ingredients for the dressing together with the hand blender except for the oil. Pour the oil in slowly so the dressing starts to bind.

4 Portion the lettuce onto 4 plates and then place the asparagus on the plates. Divide the strawberries over the plates and garnish with a slice of Parma ham. Drizzle the dressing around the salad. Serve the rest of the dressing separately.

RACK OF LAMB IN PANCETTA
WITH TOMATO ANTIBOISE

MAIN COURSE

2 racks of lamb

4 slices pancetta/smoked bacon

I tbsp olive oil

I kg (35.3oz) spinach

I clove of garlic, crushed

2 anchovy fillets

For the antibose:

2 tomatoes, seeded and diced

½ bunch of basil, cut finely

I clove of garlic, finely cut

200ml (6.8floz) olive oil

balsamic vinegar

sea salt

1   Heat the oven to 120°Celsius (248°Fahrenheit), gas mark ¼-½.

2   For the antibose, mix the tomato with the oil, basil and garlic.

3   Cut the racks into sections per three ribs. Cut out the second and third ribs and roll the meat around the remaining rib so it becomes thicker.

4   Wrap the cutlets in pancetta and bake them in the oil on all sides till they are nice and brown.

5   Allow the meat to cook for another 20 minutes in the oven.

6   Heat the oil in a pan and fry the garlic and anchovy till the anchovy has melted, stir in the spinach till reduced.

7   Put the racks of lamb on a bed of spinach and then spoon the antiboise around them. Finally, sprinkle the sauce with a little balsamic vinegar and salt.

LEMON MOUSSE

200ml (6.8floz) freshly squeezed lemon
juice, the peel of the lemon
as garnishing
6 leaves of gelatin
2 egg whites, whisked with half of the
sugar until stiff
100g (3.5oz) finely granulated sugar
300ml (10floz) whipping cream

1   Heat the lemon juice.
2   Leave the gelatin to soak till the leaves are soft, squeeze the
    water out well, and dissolve in the lemon juice.
3   Whisk the egg whites stiff with the sugar. Allow the lemon
    mixture to cool down and spoon first the cream and then the
    egg whites through it.
5   Spoon the mousse into four glasses and let it stiffen in the fridge
    for 3 hours.
6   Serve cold and garnish with grated lemon peel.

SUMMER

JUNE - JULY - AUGUST

TOMATO SOUP

500g (17.6oz) meat for the soup

1 leek, cut in rings

1 large carrot, cut in pieces

1 onion, diced

500g (17.6oz) tomatoes, diced

1 stalk of blanched celery, cut in half rings

1 sprig of lovage

3 bay leaves

1 sprig of thyme

200g (7oz) minced beef (ground beef)

a little vermicelli

pepper and salt

1   Bring the soup meat with 1½ l (50.7floz) water to the boil. Skim the water off well.

2   Add the vegetables and the herbs. Put the lid on the pan and let the stock simmer for 4 hours on a low flame. The stock does not have to boil.

3   Season the mince (ground beef) with pepper and salt and make small soup balls.

4   Sieve the stock and warm it up again, add the meatballs and the vermicelli and allow to simmer for another five minutes.

1 tbsp olive oil
1kg (35.3oz) tomatoes, finely chopped
1 clove garlic, finely chopped
small bunch of basil in slivers
700ml (23.7floz) vegetable stock

An alternative recipe:

Nowadays we do not take the time to simmer ingredients on low heat for 4 hours. That's why we will give you a faster, more modern version of tomato soup!
Heat the oil in the pan and fry the tomato and the garlic for a couple of minutes. Pour in the stock and cook the soup for 4 minutes. Stir through a sieve and add basil. All done!

CAULIFLOWER SOUP

80g (2.8oz) butter

1 blanched celery, cut into pieces

2 onions, cut into pieces

½ cauliflower, the flowerets

1l (33.8floz) vegetable stock

2 or 3 large potatoes, peeled

A small amount of celery, finely chopped

pepper and salt

1 Melt the butter in a pan and fry the blanched celery, the onions and the cauliflower flowerets lightly.

2 Pour the stock over the vegetables, add the potatoes and bring to the boil. Simmer gently till the potatoes and the vegetables are well-cooked and then purée with the hand blender. Season the soup with a little pepper and salt and garnish with the celery.

An alternative recipe:

As a rule, soup is quite an ordinary starter. However, if you present it as an amuse-gueule, you will have created something special. When you have made the soup, add 50g (1.76oz) smoked salmon (in slivers) at the last moment and serve it in small bowls. Substitute the butter with 1 tablespoon olive oil.

SHRIMP COCKTAIL

100ml (3.38floz) cream

1dl (3.38floz) mayonnaise

pinch of paprika

2 tbsp tomato ketchup

1 tbsp whisky

lemon juice

400g (14oz) (Dutch) shrimps

a few leaves of iceberg lettuce,

cut in strips

pepper and salt

250g (8.8oz) cherry tomatoes, in halves
50g (1.76oz) mixed lettuce
50g (1.76oz) marsh samphire,
rinsed with boiling water
½ cucumber, seeded and cut into half slices
To make the garlic dressing
½ bunch of parsley, cut finely
1 clove of garlic, crushed
1 egg yolk
1 tbsp white wine vinegar
100ml (3.38floz) vegetable stock
1 tbsp honey
1 tbsp maize oil

1 To make the cocktail sauce, whisk the cream in a bowl until slightly stiff then mix in the mayonnaise, paprika, ketchup and whisky. Season with a few drops of lemon juice and a little pepper and salt.

2 Rinse the shrimps under the tap with cold, running water and drain well.

3 Portion the salad into 4 coupes and heap the shrimps in the middle. Pour the cocktail sauce over the shrimps and garnish with a pinch of paprika and perhaps some parsley.

An alternative recipe:

Shrimps are very easy to combine! That's why all the ingredients in this recipe, except for the shrimps, can be changed. To make the garlic sauce, mix all the ingredients with a hand blender. Mix the shrimps with the cucumber and cherry tomatoes. Heap the shrimps on a bed of lettuce and spoon a little garlic sauce on top. Garnish with a few pieces of marsh samphire.

SPRING MASH
WITH WHITE AND GREEN BEANS

 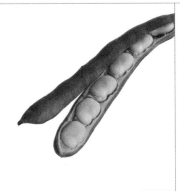

400g (14oz) floury potatoes, peeled, washed and diced

300g (10.6oz) string beans

2 frying sausages

25g (0.88oz) butter

1 jar of white beans (350g) (12.3oz)

25ml (0.85floz) milk

pepper and salt

1 Cook the potatoes and the string beans in a pan with not too much water for about 15 minutes.

2 Prick little holes in the sausages with a fork. Heat the butter in a frying pan and cook the sausages for about 10 minutes until they are nice and brown.

3 In the meantime, rinse the white beans with cold water and drain well.

4 Strain the potatoes and string beans, stir in the milk and white beans and mash everything into a smooth purée.

5 Add the frying fat and the sausages and season with salt and pepper.

6 Portion the mash into deep plates and lay the sausages on top.

An alternative recipe:

The ingredients for this dish are also tasty if they are not mashed. Mix all the ingredients coarsely together so the bits of potato are still visible. This dish is called 'naked babies in the grass' in the Netherlands and if you make it in this way, you can see why!
Add 100g (3.53oz) hazelnuts (chopped coarsely) two sprigs of rosemary and two cloves of garlic (finely chopped). Make sure it is served really warm.

ENDIVE HOTCHPOTCH

750g (26.5oz) endive, finely chopped

1½kg (53oz) potatoes,

peeled and cooked

2dl (6.8floz) milk, almost boiling

1 fresh sausage

salt and pepper

1 Heat the butter and fry the fresh sausage for about 15 minutes until it is well-cooked.

2 Mash the potatoes with milk, pepper and salt. Add the raw chopped endive and heat up again.

3 Serve the endive hotchpotch with the sausage.

An alternative recipe:

This simple recipe tastes delicious and is still made in many homes. However, it's nice to have something different from time to time.
Add 200g (7oz) smoked lardons (fried) and 100g (3.5oz) mushrooms (cut in slices). Add 1 tablespoon mustard before mashing.

CRISPY PORK BELLY SLICES

WITH POTATOES AND FRENCH BEANS

400g (14oz) pork belly slices

1 tsp mustard

1 tbsp flour

1 egg, beaten

breadcrumbs

butter

pepper and salt

1kg (35.3oz) potatoes, peeled

800g (28.2oz) French beans

1 Cook the potatoes and French beans in a pan of water.

2   Sprinkle salt and pepper onto the pork belly slices and coat them with mustard on both sides.

3 Coat both sides with flour and then with beaten egg and finally with breadcrumbs.

4 Heat the butter in the pan and fry the slices nice and brown. Be careful when frying the pork belly slices; because of the breadcrumbs they may burn quicker.

5 Portion the potatoes, vegetables and pork belly slices onto the plates.

An alternative recipe:

1 clove of garlic
1 onion, diced
1 tsp sambal
4 tbsp sweet soya sauce
1 tbsp salty soya sauce
1 tbsp lime juice

This dish is a good example of the traditional Dutch combination of cooked potatoes with vegetables and meat. The average Dutch person still eats this combination about twice a week.

Mix the ingredients for the Asian marinade. Marinate the pork belly slices for 30 minutes and fry them in a grill pan for about 10 minutes till they are done.

FRIED PLAICE

2 plaice, cleaned and dried

flour

150ml (5floz) olive oil

1 lemon cut in segments

salt

1. Rub both sides of the plaice with salt and put them in a colander so the salt can be absorbed.

2. Make a diagonal cut two or three times on the dark side of the plaice and coat the fish with flour.

3. Heat the oil in a pan and fry the plaice for 3 minutes on both sides till done, first on the light side and then on the dark side.

4. Sprinkle the fish with the juice from the segments of lemon.

An alternative recipe:

Fried plaice is often eaten in coastal areas, but this fish is also very tasty when prepared in the oven. Heat the oven to 180° Celsius (356°Fahrenheit), gas mark 4-5. Cut the plaice in half lengthwise, beat them flat and fill them with 2 tomatoes (cut into pieces), 100g (3.53oz) spinach and 1 clove of garlic (crushed). Roll the plaice up and put them in the oven for about 10 minutes till they are done.

STEAK
WITH MUSHROOM SAUCE

4 Steaks

40g (1.4oz) butter

3 tbsp oil

freshly ground pepper

salt

1 small onion, shredded

100g (3.53oz) mushrooms, halved

2 tbsp flour

200ml (6.8floz) milk

1   Sprinkle both sides of the steak with pepper.

2   Heat the butter and the oil in a pan till it has browned. Fry the steak for about 3 minutes on both sides.

3   For the mushroom sauce; fry the onion and the mushrooms in a pan till they start to brown.

4   Add a little flour so the liquid of the mushrooms and the butter is soaked up.

5   Pour in the milk slowly till you have a nice thick sauce. Make sure the milk has been absorbed before you add the next dash.

6   Season the sauce with a little pepper and salt.

7   Take the meat out of the pan and sprinkle with salt before serving. Give the sauce separately.

An alternative recipe:

Dutch mothers used to fry steaks in very hot butter and slide the steaks slowly over the bottom of the pan to seal the meat well on all sides. This is still the best way to prepare a steak. Do not prod a fork into the meat as this will make the meat less tender. Stir-fry the slices of steak together with 200g (7oz) of shiitake mushrooms (torn into pieces) and 1 clove of garlic (crushed) in 1 tablespoon of olive oil. Sprinkle with pepper and salt. Lovely and crispy!

FRIED SALMON
WITH HOLLANDAISE SAUCE

4 salmon fillets,

each about 150g (5.3oz)

lemon juice

flour

75g (2.6oz) butter

50g (1.76oz) shallots, shredded

200g (7.1oz) butter, melted

50ml (1.69floz) vinegar

50ml (1.69floz) water

3 egg yolks

10 white peppercorns

juice of half a lemon

pinch of cayenne pepper

salt

2 leeks
50ml (1.7floz) fish stock
50ml (1.7floz) white wine
salt

1. Sprinkle the salmon fillets with salt and then with lemon juice.
2. Coat the fillets with flour and then shake off the surplus flour.
3. Heat the butter in a frying pan and fry the salmon on both sides for about 4 minutes till cooked.
4. To make the hollandaise sauce, mix the shallots, vinegar, 50ml (1.69floz) water and the peppercorns together in a pan. Put this on high heat and bring to the boil.
5. Reduce the mixture to half its volume and stir it through a sieve. Allow to cool till below 50° Celsius (122° Fahrenheit).
6. Add the egg yolks and whisk this mixture au-bain-marie till it binds.
7. Take the pan out of the water and add the butter, keep whisking.
8. Season the sauce with lemon juice, cayenne pepper and salt.
9. Portion the salmon onto plates and serve with the sauce.

An alternative recipe:

Fish is very healthy due to the Omega 3 fatty acids. However, this dish can be even healthier by leaving out the calorie rich sauce and steaming it in the oven. Preheat the oven to 180°Celsius (356° Fahrenheit), gas mark 4-5. Cook the leek briefly in a pan with the wine and fish stock. Put the leek with the liquid on a piece of aluminium foil and lay the salmon fillet on top. Sprinkle with salt, fold up the foil and then put the salmon packages in the oven for about 20 minutes till they are cooked.

RHUBARB

500g (17.6oz) rhubarb, stalks cut into pieces of 2 cm (0.75inch)

50ml (1.7floz) orange juice

castor sugar

1   Cook the rhubarb for a few minutes with the orange juice.

2   Let the rhubarb cool and then flavour it with a little castor sugar.

An alternative recipe:

Grandma's golden rule with this dessert used to be: 'always cook it with a piece of chalk'. Rhubarb contains a lot of oxalic acid that extracts calcium from the body. A small piece of chalk (or egg shells) neutralizes this effect.
Cook two apples (peeled and in pieces), 250g (8.8oz) strawberries (in halves) and 2 tablespoons strawberry liqueur along with the orange juice. This gives the sour rhubarb a clean taste and makes it easier to eat.

REDCURRANT DELIGHT

300ml (10floz) red current juice

3 egg whites

75g (2.6oz) sugar

salt

1   Mix the red current juice with the egg whites, sugar and a little salt till the mixture is stiff but airy.

2   Portion the dessert into four bowls and serve with a biscuit if so desired.

An alternative recipe:

Mix 200g (7oz) of black currents and 200g (7oz) of red currents in with the red current juice. Add 2 tablespoons of black current liqueur. Keep a few nice branches for garnishing. Now this simple dessert is no longer simple but very festive. It can also be served with whipped cream.

SUMMER MENU

STIR-FRIED TUNA FISH — BERGYLT FILLET — WHITE WINE SABAYON

STIR-FRIED TUNA FISH
WITH PEA PURÉE

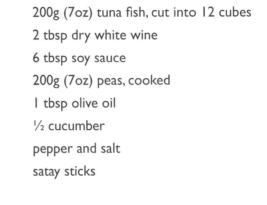

200g (7oz) tuna fish, cut into 12 cubes

2 tbsp dry white wine

6 tbsp soy sauce

200g (7oz) peas, cooked

1 tbsp olive oil

½ cucumber

pepper and salt

satay sticks

1   Marinate the tuna cubes in the wine and the soy sauce for approx. 30 minutes. Keep the marinade.

2   Cook the peas and purée them using the hand blender. Add the olive oil while mixing and season with pepper and salt.

3   Slice 8 thin slivers from the cucumber with the cheese slicer.

4   Heat the oil in a wok, make sure it is very hot and stir fry the tuna on all sides.

5   Thread three bits of tuna and three bits of cucumber onto a satay stick. Make three rounds of purée on a plate and put the skewer on the rounds.

6   Serve the remaining marinade separately.

BERGYLT FILLET
WITH COURGETTE SPAGHETTI

4 pieces of bergylt with skin,
about 120g (4.2oz) each

1 tbsp olive oil

2 cloves of garlic, finely chopped

2 courgettes, in very thin strips

2 tomatoes, seeded and sliced into strips

2 tbsp black olives

salt

1. Heat the oil in a pan and fry the bergylt for 1 minute, turn it over and fry on low heat on the skin side till done, sprinkle with salt.
2. Cut the strips of courgette into thin strings.
3. Fry the garlic briefly in another pan, add the tomato, olives and courgette, and fry for 1 minute.
4. Portion the courgette spaghetti onto 4 plates, lay the bergylt on top and pour the oil mixture from the pan over it.

WHITE WINE SABAYON

WITH FRESH SUMMER FRUIT

200g (7oz) strawberries

200g (7oz) bilberries (blueberries)

200g (70z) red currents

200g (7oz) raspberries

200g (7oz) blackberries

To make the sabayon

4 egg yolks

50g (1.76oz) sugar

2 dl (6.8floz) dry white wine

1   Portion the fruit onto four plates.

2   Whisk the egg yolks with a whisk or hand blender in
    a bowl together with the sugar and wine till it becomes
    a stiff white mixture.

3   Place the bowl in a pan with boiling water so the bottom of the
    bowl does not touch the water (au bain marie). Keep on whisking
    the mixture till it is so stiff that it no longer runs out.

4   Spoon the sabayon over the fruit and serve directly.

AUTUMN

SEPTEMBER - OCTOBER - NOVEMBER

MUSHROOM SOUP

1 tbsp lemon juice

250g (8.8oz) mushrooms, sliced

4 tbsp butter

1 onion, shredded

½ tsp marjoram

100ml (3.38floz) dry white wine

700 ml (23.7floz) vegetable stock

200ml (6.8floz) semi-skimmed milk

2 tbsp flour

pepper, freshly ground

1 Drizzle the lemon juice over the mushrooms.

2 Heat two tablespoons of butter in a pan and fry the onions in this. Add the mushrooms and fry these together with the onions for a little while.

3 Stir in the marjoram, wine, vegetable stock and milk and let it simmer for approx. 15 minutes.

4 Let the stock cool down.

5 Melt the rest of the butter in another pan, stir in the flour and pour the stock little by little into the pan (the soup should be brought to the boil each time).

6 Season with salt and pepper.

An alternative recipe:

Creamy mushroom soup is one of the classic soups. If you like mushrooms but not creamy soup, then why not make a clear one? This is an even healthier alternative.
Bring 900ml (30.4floz) vegetable stock to the boil together with 100ml (3.38floz) sherry. Add 400g (14oz) mushrooms and a pinch of finely chopped parsley and simmer for 4 minutes.

CELERIAC SOUP

250g (8.8oz) celeriac, cut into cubes

15g (0.5oz) butter

the white of 1 leek, cut into rings

1 small potato, peeled, in cubes

1 sprig of thyme

1 sprig of rosemary

500ml (17floz) vegetable stock

40g (1.4oz) mushrooms, cleaned and cut into slices

1 Melt the butter in a pan and sauté the leek, celeriac, and potato.

2 Add the thyme, rosemary and stock. Bring everything to the boil, cover the pan with a lid and let the vegetables cook gently. Use a hand blender to purée the soup and then strain it.

3 Add the mushrooms and simmer for another 2 minutes.

4 Season with salt and pepper.

An alternative recipe:

Celeriac is a vegetable which should be judged on its own merits. A lot of people only use the root vegetable in soups. However, the celeriac is aromatic, has a delicious flavour and a lot of minerals (phosphor and calcium). It is a very healthy vegetable and not in the least expensive. Add a little Danish Blue Castello cheese at the very last minute and it becomes a very trendy soup.

VOL-AU-VENTS

WITH MUSHROOM RAGOUT

4 vol-au-vent puff pastry cases

250g (8.8oz) fresh mushrooms, sliced

500ml (17floz) vegetable stock

1 tbsp butter

2 tbsp flour

1 tbsp parsley, finely chopped

2 tbsp sour cream

pepper and salt

1   Put the pastry cases in a hot oven.

2   Cook the mushrooms in the stock and let them cool.

3   Heat the butter, add the flour and keep stirring till all the flour is absorbed by the butter.

4   Stir a little cold stock gradually into this mixture and keep on stirring to prevent lumps.

5   Finally, add the rest of the stock together with the mushrooms and simmer for 5 minutes on low heat.

6   Just before serving, stir the parsley, sour cream and a little pepper and salt into the ragout.

7   Fill the vol-au-vents with the ragout, put the lids back on and serve directly.

FILO PASTRY POUCHES
WITH MUSHROOMS

An alternative recipe:

1 tbsp butter

1 tbsp flour

2 tbsp melted butter

8 sheets of filo pastry

1 tbsp olive oil

200g (7oz) mixed mushrooms,
torn into large pieces

2 cloves of garlic, finely chopped

 pinch of parsley, finely chopped

1 tbsp mustard

1 leek leaf

salt and pepper

1   Preheat the oven to 200°Celsius
     (400° Fahrenheit), gas mark 6.

2   Coat 4 sheets of filo pastry with the melted
      butter and lay another sheet of filo pastry on
      top; use a rolling pin to roll the sheets together.

3   Heat the olive oil in a pan and fry the
     mushrooms till the liquid evaporates.

4   Add the butter, garlic, parsley and mustard and
     fry all these ingredients for 1 minute, sprinkle
     with salt and pepper.

5   Divide the mushroom mixture over the filo
     mixture and tie the pouches with a thin leek
     ribbon.

Filo pastry originates from the Middle-East. It is thinner
than puff pastry and crispier when baked. It also has less
fat!

MEAT STEW

500g (17.6oz) stewing steak
or 600g-750g (21oz-26oz) marbled
braising steak at room temperature
butter
1 large onion, coarsely chopped
3 tbsp vinegar
3 bay leaves
2 cloves
1 tbsp cornflour/starch if necessary
pepper and salt

1 red pepper, seeded and in thin rings
2 black olives, without stones
200g (7oz) chorizo, cut in cubes
4 cloves of garlic, finely chopped
200ml (6.8floz) red wine
sprig of thyme
sprig of rosemary

1   Season the meat with pepper and salt. Heat the butter in a pan and fry the meat till it is sealed on one side and is nicely browned. Take the meat out of the pan.

2   Lightly brown the onion in the left over fat. Add 200ml (6.8floz) water, vegetable stock, vinegar, bay leaf and cloves and bring everything to the boil.

3   Put the meat in the stock and subsequently bring everything to the boil again. Simmer on low heat for about 3 to 3 ½ hours with the lid on the pan. If necessary, add water if the top pieces of meat are under less than half the vegetable stock. Turn the meat over half way through the cooking time. When done, take the meat out of the pan and allow it to drain.

4   To make tasty gravy, sieve the stock well and then bring it to the boil. Mix it with a combination of cornflour and water.

An alternative recipe:

Once, the smell of stewing meat permeated the house on rainy Saturdays. That gave a cosy, homely feeling. If you are in a nostalgic mood and have enough time, it is a really good idea to make a meat stew.
If you want to give it your own signature, you can use the ingredients mentioned opposite.

CHOW MEIN

400g (14oz) Chinese noodles

3 tbsp olive oil

300g (10.6oz) pork steak,

cut into small pieces

1 leek, in rings

1 onion, diced

200g (7oz) white or savoy cabbage

3 cloves of garlic, crushed

200g (7oz) cooked ham,

cut into small pieces

1 tbsp soy sauce

1   Prepare the Chinese noodles as stated on the package and drain
    after cooking.

2   Heat the oil in a wok and stir fry the pork steak till it is nice
    and brown.

3   Add the leek, cabbage and garlic and stir fry everything till cooked
    but still firm.

4   Stir the Chinese noodles, ham and ketchup through the
    vegetables and stir fry everything well for another 5 minutes.
    This dish also tastes good served with slivers of omelette.

½ oxheart cabbage, finely chopped
1 onion, diced
200g shrimps
100g bean sprouts
2 eggs, added and fried along
with the rest of the ingredients

An alternative recipe:

The savoy cabbage is one of the oldest cabbage varieties
in the world. This white cabbage keeps our resistance
and mineral requirements up to standard in the winter.
It used to be food for the poor, but it now has a wealth
of culinary uses. Do you make Chow Mein the same way
time after time and are you in need of a change? Stir fry
the following ingredients briefly in the pan and serve with
the Chinese noodles. Fast and delicious!

SIZZLING HOT APPLE

AND BACON MASH

300g (10.6oz) smoked bacon

1 kg (35.3oz) potatoes, peeled and cut into small pieces

500g (17.6oz) sweet apples, peeled, without the core and cut in quarters

500g (17.6oz) sour apples, peeled, without the core and cut in quarters

1   Cook the bacon for 30 minutes in a large amount of boiling water.

2   Add the potatoes and lay the sweet apples on top of these. Make another layer by adding the sour apples. Cook everything for about 20 minutes till ready.

3   Pour the water off, take out the bacon and cut this into slices.

4   Mash the potatoes and the apples together, put the bacon on top and serve sizzling hot.

An alternative recipe:

This recipe is really sizzling hot because of the apples. The liquid from the apples becomes very hot during cooking. This means that you can easily burn your mouth during eating. If you wish, you can also cut the meat into cubes and mix this with the potatoes and apples. Or use pears instead of apples, but be careful while eating, you have been forewarned!

RED CABBAGE

1 kg (35.3oz) red cabbage,
cut into small pieces
1 onion, diced
dash of red wine vinegar
1 tbsp castor sugar
knob of butter
3 bay leaves
3 cloves
1 tsp cinnamon
2 apples, peeled and in cubes
100ml (3.38floz) red wine
200ml (6.8floz) vegetable stock
salt

1   Mix the cabbage and the onions together with the other ingredients in a pan. Cook the cabbage for 60 minutes on low heat.

2   Remove the bay leaves and cloves.

3   Delicious combined with Dutch stew and mashed potato (see page 122)

An alternative recipe:

Cooking is searching for the ultimate taste experience. If you make this version you can be certain that your guests will be in for a surprise! Fry the following ingredients in a pan and add the cooked red cabbage: 1 red pepper (seeded and cut in thin slices). 1cm (0.39inch) ginger (grated), 2 cloves of garlic (crushed), 2 tablespoons of peanuts (unsalted), 1 tablespoon of brown sugar.

DUTCH STYLE SAUERKRAUT

300g (10.6oz) lean bacon

750g (26.5oz) sauerkraut

1½ kg (53oz) potatoes, cooked

100ml (3.38floz) milk

salt and pepper

1   Cook the bacon for 15 minutes in 100ml (3.38floz) water.

2   Add the sauerkraut and potatoes and simmer together.

3   Mash all the ingredients well. Make sure the dish is nice and hot before serving.

An alternative recipe:

Traditional Dutch recipes used to have fewer ingredients than nowadays. If you want a fancier recipe, why not use salmon? Serve this 'stamppot' (mash) with 4 salmon fillets, each about 120g (4.25oz). Put them in a pan and fry them on both sides for approx. 5 minutes. Cook the bacon with 100ml (3.38floz) orange juice and add a small amount of finely chopped mint at the last minute.

CHICORY AU GRATIN
WITH HAM AND CHEESE

8 heads chicory (Belgian endive), the
bitter parts removed
8 slices of ham
8 slices of semi-matures cheese
25g (0.88oz) butter
a few drops of lemon juice
salt

1   Preheat the oven to 200°Celsius (400° Fahrenheit), gas mark 6.

2   Cook the chicory till almost done in a small amount of salted
    water. This takes about 20 minutes.

3   Strain the chicory, wrap the vegetable first in slices of ham and
    then in slices of cheese.

4   Carefully transfer to a greased baking dish large enough to snugly
    hold the chicory. Put the dish in the preheated oven until the
    cheese turns a golden brown (approx. 5 minutes). Serve hot.

An alternative recipe:

In olden days, cows and pigs were slaughtered in November.
Their meat was made into sausages, bacon or salted meat.
A lot of the meat that was eaten in this month needed a
bitter counterpart. Chicory or Belgian endive as it is also
known, fitted the bill. Chicory can also be caramelized. Melt
100g (3.5oz) sugar in a pan together with half a tablespoon
of butter and then add 100ml (3.38floz) orange juice. Add
the raw chicory (in pieces cut at an angle) as soon as the
sugar has dissolved and cook for 1 minute in the mixture.

PLUM DUFF

500ml (17floz) milk

50g (1.76oz) yeast

300g (10.6oz) flour

2 eggs, lightly beaten

50g (1.76oz) sugar

75g (2.6oz) raisins

75g (2.6oz) currents

75g (2.6oz) candied peel

syrup (molasses)

salt

1 Warm 2 tablespoons of milk in a small pan and mix it together with the yeast. Spoon the flour into a dish, make a hollow in the flour and add the yeast mixture.

2 Add the eggs, milk, sugar and a pinch of salt and knead everything together till it becomes an airy dough. Add the raisins, currents and candied peel.

3 Spoon the batter into a white cotton bag (or tea towel) that has been dusted with flower. Close and tie the bag but not too tightly as the dough still has to rise.

4 Put the bag on a saucer in a pan with lukewarm water (this is to prevent it getting burnt). Bring to the boil slowly and cook for 2½ hours.

5 Take the plum duff out of the bag and cut it into slices using a wire. Serve with syrup.

An alternative recipe:

Plum duff is an old country recipe and is called 'Jan in de zak ' (John in the bag) in the Netherlands for obvious reasons. It was only eaten when the weather was cold because it is filling and has a warming effect. That was exactly what was needed on the farm.
The currents and raisins can be replaced by fresh fruit.

BUTTERMILK PORRIDGE
WITH SYRUP

DESSERT

100g (3.53oz) wheat flour

1l (33.8floz) buttermilk

salt

syrup (molasses)

granulated sugar

1   Mix the flour in a pan with a small amount of buttermilk. Keep stirring till all the lumps have gone and a thick, smooth mixture remains.

2   Add the remaining buttermilk gradually and stir the mixture well so it does not form lumps.

3   Flavour the buttermilk porridge with a little salt and keep on stirring till it is cooked. This takes about 10 minutes.

4   Serve the porridge with sugar and syrup.

An alternative recipe:

Up in the north of the Netherlands, in the province of Groningen, this was called Soup Porridge ('Zoepenbrij'). Accordingly, the church clock that chimed at twelve 'o clock was called the 'Zoepenbrij' clock as the noonday meal was eaten at that time.
Soak 250g (8.8oz) of dried figs for 30 minutes in red port. Cook the figs in the buttermilk. The red colour of the port blends with the buttermilk and the dessert subsequently becomes red.

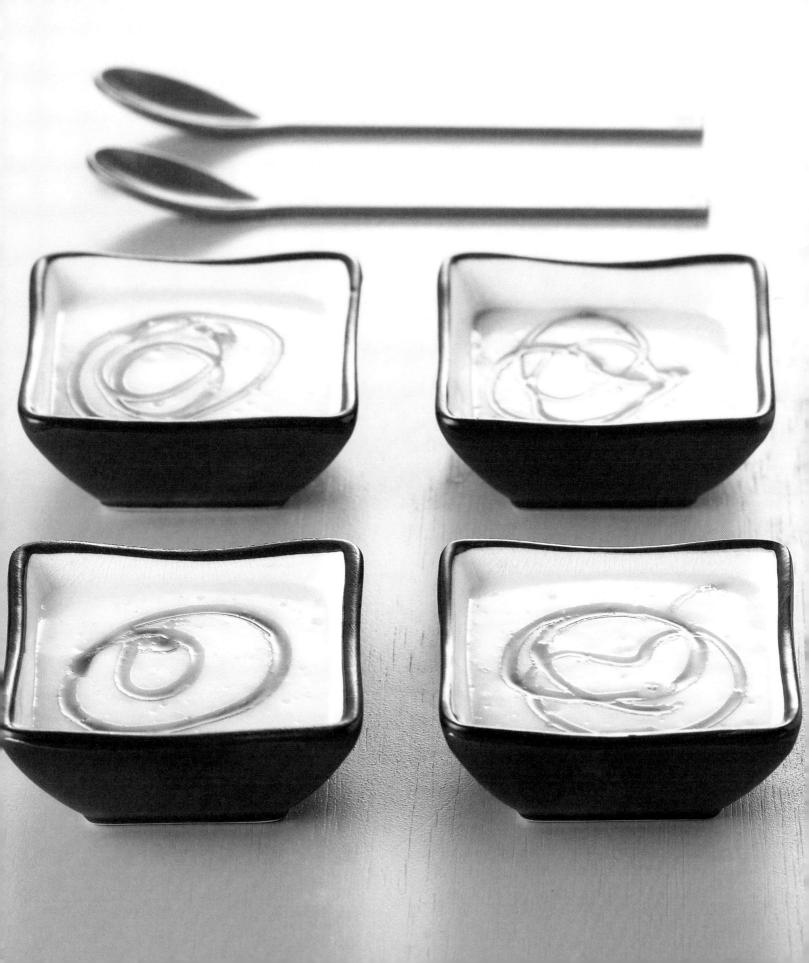

AUTUMN MENU

MUSHROOM SALAD- RABBIT WITH BEANS- CHEESECAKE

MUSHROOM SALAD
WITH TRUFFLE OIL DRESSING

250g (8.8oz) mixed mushrooms

½ tbsp butter

80g (2.8oz) mixed lettuce

2 tomatoes, seeded and in slices

I tbsp walnuts, coarsely chopped

To make the dressing

I tsp mustard

I tsp white wine vinegar

I tsp honey

I egg yolk

I tbsp vegetable stock

I tbsp truffle oil

4 tbsp maize oil

1   Mix all the ingredients for the dressing, except for the maize oil, together with a hand blender;

2   Add the oil drop by drop and whisk the mixture till it becomes homogeneous. Season with a little salt if necessary.

3   Fry the mushrooms in a hot dry pan. Shake loose till all the liquid has evaporated. Only then, add the butter.

4   Fry for another couple of minutes, season with salt and pepper.

5   Portion the lettuce onto 4 plates and spoon the mushroom mixture over the leaves. Add the walnuts and tomatoes. Drizzle the dressing around the salad and serve with extra dressing on the side.

RABBIT WITH BEANS
AND BEER

2 tbsp olive oil

4 legs of rabbit

2 sprigs of sage, finely chopped

3 shallots, finely chopped

1 clove of garlic, diced

2 bay leaves

1 bottle of beer

1 jar of game stock

30 silver onions

150g (5.3oz) dried white beans, soaked
overnight

150g (5.3oz) dried marrowfat beans,
soaked overnight

150g (5.3oz) peas

salt

1   Heat the oil in the pan and fry the legs of rabbit for a couple of
    minutes, add the sage, shallots, garlic and bay leaf.

2   Let it cook for 4 minutes and then add the beer and the stock.
    Finally, add the white beans, the marrowfat beans and the peas.
    Cook for approx. 1 minute.

3   Heat well and simmer for 90 minutes (check if the rabbit is ready,
    if not, cook a little longer).

4   Put the silver onions in during the last five minutes and stew for
    a few minutes more.

CHEESECAKE
WITH ORANGE AND ALMONDS

160g (5.64oz) soft butter

120g (4.23oz) sugar

500g (17.6oz) mascarpone

400g (14oz) cottage cheese

6 eggs, separated

grated rind of 4 oranges

200g (7oz) almonds

150g (5.3oz) flour, sieved

300g (10.6oz) white chocolate, grated or

in small pieces

1 round spring form baking tin of 26cm

(10.25 inch) diameter.

1   Preheat the oven to 180° (356° Fahrenheit), gas mark 4.

2   Mix the butter with the sugar until it turns white and creamy.

3   Whisk the egg yolks and stir them into the butter mixture together with the mascarpone, cottage cheese, orange rind, almonds and flour.

4   Whisk the egg whites until they are stiff and spoon them, together with the chocolate, through the mixture.

5   Spoon the mixture into the baking tin and place it in the middle of the oven.

6   Bake the cake for about 50 minutes. Prick in the middle with a satay stick: if the stick is dry, the cake is ready.

7   Turn off the oven; leave the cake in the oven with the door open for five minutes. Then dust with powdered sugar.

8   When the cake has cooled, cut it into wedges. It tastes best when still lukewarm.

WINTER

DECEMBER - JANUARY - FEBRUARY

PEA SOUP

300g (10.6oz) dried green peas

200g (7oz) dried split peas

500g (17.6oz) pork spareribs

1 smoked pork hock

250g (8.8oz) smoked pork cheek bacon, in slices

3-4 leeks, sliced in pieces

1 celeriac, cut into pieces

2 large bunches of celery, finely chopped

2 smoked sausages

salt

1 Soak the peas for at least 12 hours in approx. 3l (101floz) water.

2 Bring the peas, meat and bacon to the boil in the water used for soaking. Keep at boiling point for 2 hours and regularly skim off the water.

3 Season with salt and add the leek and celeriac. Simmer for another hour on low heat.

4 Take the meat and the bacon out of the soup. Remove the bones and put the meat back in the soup together with the bacon.

5 Rub the peas fine against the side of the pan and then simmer the soup on low heat. Stir regularly to prevent a crust forming on the bottom of the pan.

6 Add the celery shortly before serving. Simmer the sausages in a separate pan and when ready, cut into slices. Put the slices in the soup.

An alternative recipe:

From generation to generation the haybox was used to cook food after it had been brought to the boil elsewhere (it was also used to keep food warm). This was only possibly with food that could cook itself, such as pea soup, rice pudding etc. Pea soup tastes best when made in large quantities and kept for a day before consumption. If you like spicy soup, pop a red pepper (seeded, cut into small rings) and 2 tablespoons of soy sauce into the soup a few minutes before serving.

OXTAIL SOUP

1 kg (35.3oz) oxtail cut into pieces

2 tbsp tomato purée

2 onions, cut into rings

1 large carrot, cut into pieces

10 black peppercorns

2 cloves

2 bay leaves

a little mace

2 sprigs of thyme, finely chopped

6 sprigs of celery, finely chopped

pinch of finely chopped parsley

pinch of finely chopped chives

pepper and salt

1   Heat the soup in a large pan and fry the oxtail brown on all sides.

2   Add the tomato purée and fry with the oxtail for about
    2 minutes.

3   Pour 1½ (51 floz) litres of water into the pan and bring to the boil.
    Regularly skim off the water.

4   Stir in the onions, carrots and herbs and simmer for about
    3½ hours.

5   Strain the soup and remove the meat from the bones.
    Season with a little pepper and salt and return to the soup.

6   Sprinkle fresh herbs over the soup before serving.

An alternative recipe:

Oxtail soup is made from the tail of the ox. This has a lot of
taste and can make strong soups. If you cook the oxtail on
low heat for a long time it becomes tender and falls off the
bone. This can be used in the soup.
Add a little coriander and 2 tablespoons of soy sauce before
serving. The soup now tastes really surprising!

COOKING PEARS

8 small cooking pears, peeled in quarters

juice from ½ lemon

75g (2.7oz) sugar

About 4 cm lemon rind

1 cinnamon stick

2 cloves

1 tbsp red wine vinegar

2 dl (6.76floz) red wine

1. Sprinkle the pears with the lemon juice to stop them discolouring.
2. Bring 2dl (6.76floz) water and the wine and sugar, lemon juice, cinnamon, cloves and vinegar to the boil.
3. Turn the heat down low and put the pears upright and next to each other in the pan. Add cold water till the pears are three quarters under water. Simmer in this way for 30-40 minutes on low heat or till the pears are soft.
4. Take the pears out of the pan and keep them covered and warm.
5. Remove the lemon rind, the cinnamon stick and the cloves and cook the remaining liquid on high heat till it becomes syrupy.
6. Pour the liquid over the pears just before serving.

An alternative recipe:

This typical Dutch side dish was often put on the table at Christmas. Although granny's pears are the best, there is nothing to stop you having a go yourself!
Use white wine instead of red, a little star anise and 2 tablespoons of Drambuie liqueur. Use pears with nice stalks, peel them but keep them whole and leave the stalks. Serve with the syrup poured over the pears.

HARE STEW

approx. 1½ kg (53oz) hare joints

100g (3.53oz) butter

100g (3.53oz) thick bacon, in cubes

2 tbsp tomato purée

flour

300ml (10floz) red wine

1 tbsp black current syrup

1 onion, finely chopped

½ large carrot, finely chopped

3 cloves

2 bay leaves

4 to 6 black peppercorns, crushed

pepper and salt

1   Rub the hare joints with pepper and salt.

2   Heat the butter in a large pan and brown the pieces of hare on all sides.

3   Add the bacon and fry for a couple of minutes.

4   Now stir in the tomato purée and sprinkle the meat with a little flour.

5   Add the wine and black current syrup and bring to a boil.

6   Add the onion, carrot, cloves and peppercorns. Simmer for approx. 1½ hours with the lid on the pan.

7   Cut the meat off the bone, put it back in the pan and season the hare stew with salt and pepper.

An alternative recipe:

Hare stew is a real Christmas dish in the Netherlands. You may find the shot that killed the animal or you may be the lucky one to find the wish bone. Two people pull the bone apart and whoever ends up with the longest bit, makes a wish. Add the following ingredients when you get to point 7: 2 slices of spice cake, 200g (7oz) mushrooms, 1 tablespoon of syrup. Allow to simmer for 5 minutes. Garnish with a little parsley.

MUSSELS

4 kg (141oz) mussels

2 onions in rings

1 leek, in rings

1 large carrot, cut into pieces

4 sprigs of celery

4 sprigs of parsley

4 sprigs of thyme, chopped finely

3 cloves garlic

6 bay leaves

1 tbsp pepper corns

500ml (17floz) amber coloured beer

1 Wash the mussels well in cold water. All the mussels should be closed. If not, tap the mussels that have an open shell, if they still do not shut, throw them away.

2 Put the mussels in a large pan with a little water at the bottom and add all the other ingredients.

3 Close the pan with a lid and bring to the boil.
Toss the mussels regularly.

4 The mussels are ready when all the shells are open.

An alternative recipe:

Shellfish are never eaten raw, except for oysters. They often have parasites so be careful when preparing and eating shellfish. Those that rise to the top of the water when rinsed or have broken shells or shells that do not open, should be thrown away.

To give this recipe a different taste, use 200ml (6.8floz) of wine instead of beer and add two tablespoons of Chilli sauce and 1 red pepper (finely chopped) to the mussels.

HUNTER'S STYLE HOTPOT

600g (21oz) stewing steak (or lean braising steak), cut into cubes

flour

100g (3.53oz) butter

1 tbsp bacon fat

1 large onion, shredded

1 sour apple, peeled and cut into small pieces

3 cloves

2 bay leaves

10 juniper berries, crushed

10 silver onions, pickled

200ml (6.76floz) red wine, warm

mashed potato made from 1 kg (35.3oz) potatoes

2 (Dutch) rusks, crumbled

pepper and salt

1. Preheat the oven to 200° Celsius (400° Fahrenheit), gas mark 6.
2. Dust the meat with flour. Heat the bacon fat and half the butter in a pan and fry the meat on both sides till it is golden brown.
3. Add the onion and the apple and brown these in the fat.
4. Stir in the cloves, bay leaves, silver onions and a little pepper and salt and pour the wine over these ingredients. Mix everything together well and simmer on low heat for about 3 hours. If necessary, add boiling water if the mixture gets too dry.
5. When ready, put the meat and the onions together with the liquid in a casserole and cover everything with a layer of mashed potatoes. Sprinkle with rusk crumbs and divide the remaining butter over the dish.
6. Put the dish in the oven and cook till the hotpot has a golden brown crust.

An alternative recipe:

Nowadays (grand) parents disapprove of throwing leftovers into the rubbish bin. Nothing was thrown away in the olden days, they had a leftovers day. This hotpot is a luxury version of a dish that was made when potatoes and meat were left over. Before covering the meat with the mashed potatoes, you could mix in a tablespoon of mustard, 1 sprig of thyme, 1 mace leaf and 200g (7oz) mushrooms (halved).

CARROT HOTCHPOTCH

WITH BEEF BRISKET

800g (28oz) beef brisket

1l (33.8floz) vegetable stock

8 onions cut into rings

8 large carrots, washed and cleaned

1kg (35.3oz) potatoes, peeled and washed

4 tsp mustard

pepper and salt

1   Cook the brisket for about 1½ hours in the vegetable stock. When done, let it cool and cut it into (not too thin) slices.

2   Cook the onions and carrots for 30 minutes, the potatoes for 20 minutes.

3   Strain the carrots, onions and potatoes, mash them and season with pepper and salt.

An alternative recipe:

Brisket is interspersed with strings of fat which gives it a characteristic flavour. This hotchpotch can also be given an Eastern twist by adding 100g (3.53oz) coconut (grated), 1cm 0.39inch) ginger (grated) 200ml (6.76floz) coconut milk and a sprinkling of (finely cut) coriander.

DUTCH STEW
WITH MASHED POTATOES

500g (7.6oz) chuck steak, cut into small
pieces

60g (2oz) butter

3 onions, in rings

2 tbsp vinegar

6g (0.25oz) sugar

6 cloves

3 bay leaves

50g (1.76oz) smoked bacon

pepper and salt

1   Season the chuck steak with a little pepper and salt.

2   Heat the butter in the pan and cook the pieces of chuck steak till
    nicely browned.

3   Add the onions when the meat has browned and cook till glassy.
    Pour in enough water for everything to be just under water.

4   Add the vinegar, sugar, cloves and bay leaves and simmer for
    2½ hours.

5   Take the cloves and bay leaf out of the pan, add the smoked
    bacon and simmer for another half hour.

6   If necessary bind the liquid with a thickener.

An alternative recipe:

This Dutch stew was always eaten with red cabbage (see
page 88). Both dishes go together so well, that there is no
better combination conceivable.
When adding the herbs, you can also put in a few drops
of Tabasco, 2 slices of spice cake (or gingerbread) and
1 tablespoon of apple spread.

CURLY KALE
WITH SMOKED SAUSAGE

600g (21oz) curly kale, finely chopped

1kg (35.3oz) potatoes, peeled, in pieces

1 fresh smoked sausage

1½ dl (5floz) milk

35g (1.25oz) butter

1 tbsp mustard

salt

1   Cook the curly kale for about 10 minutes in a pan with a little water.

2   Put the potatoes in a large pan, divide the pre-cooked curly kale over them and put the sausage on top. Cook everything for about 30 minutes till done.

3   Mash the curly kale together with the potatoes, milk, butter and mustard and season the hotchpotch with salt.

5   Cut the sausage into slices and serve these together with the hotchpotch.

An alternative recipe:

If making a hotchpotch is no longer a challenge, go Italian! Substitute the smoked sausage for a spicy Italian sausage such as Cacciatore.
Stir pieces of Cacciatore sausage, sun-dried tomato (finely chopped) and 1 onion through the Curly kale hotchpotch and heat everything well before serving.

SEMOLINA PUDDING

WITH REDCURRANT JUICE

I lemon rind, grated

I lemon rind

1l (33.8floz) full cream milk

85g (3oz) semolina

125g (4.5oz) sugar

½ cinnamon stick

I small bottle of red current juice

I level tbsp potato starch

1   Bring the milk with the grated lemon rind to the boil in a pan and simmer for 5 minutes.

2   Mix the semolina with 75g (2.6oz) sugar and add this to the boiling milk. Cook for approx. 7 minutes, keep stirring.

3   Rinse the inside of a pudding mould (volume approx. 1l (33.8floz)) with cold water and pour the liquid into the mould. Let the pudding cool and stiffen.

4   Meanwhile, bring 100ml (3.38floz) water, the cinnamon stick and the lemon rind to the boil. Add the current juice and the remaining sugar and bring to the boil again.

5   Mix the potato starch with 5 tablespoons of water into a smooth mixture and add it to the current juice. Stir well till it binds.

6   Take the lemon rind and the cinnamon stick out of the sauce and allow to cool.

7   Turn the pudding mould over onto a dish and serve with the sauce poured over the pudding.

An alternative recipe:

Use ½l (17floz) coconut milk and ½l (17floz) semi-skimmed milk. Instead of just using sugar, use 100g (3.53oz) coconut and 40g (1.4oz) sugar. Garnish the pudding with 250g (8.8oz) red currents instead of red current juice.

BACON PANCAKES
WITH SYRUP

2 eggs, whisked

250g (8.8oz) wholemeal or buckwheat flour

100ml (3.38floz) milk

150ml (5floz) water, lukewarm

pinch of salt

butter for frying

16 rashers of bacon

syrup

1   Mix the eggs, flour and half the milk together in a bowl and make a smooth batter. Subsequently, add the remaining milk and water and the pinch of salt.

2   Heat the butter in a frying pan, pour a spoonful of batter into the pan and let it spread out nicely.

3   Portion 4 rashers of bacon onto the batter and fry the pancake light brown on both sides.

4   Serve the pancake with syrup.

An alternative recipe:

3 sweet red peppers, roasted
150ml (5floz) milk
90g (3.2oz) self rising flour
3 eggs
2 tbsp olive oil
500g (17.6oz) mixed vegetables for stir-frying

A crêpe is a paper-thin pancake. The following is, in a nutshell, the recipe for 'Crêpes made from roasted sweet peppers with stir-fried vegetables'. Purée the sweet pepper with the milk and add the eggs and flour while constantly stirring. Keep on stirring till you have a smooth batter. Put aside and let it rest for 30 minutes. Heat the oil in a pan and make 4 large crêpes with the batter. Stir fry the vegetables, fill the crêpes with the vegetables and fold them up.

WINTER MENU

HAKE FILLET- FILLED ROLLED BEEF- WHITE CHOCOLATE MOUSSE

HAKE FILLET
FILLED WITH SALMON

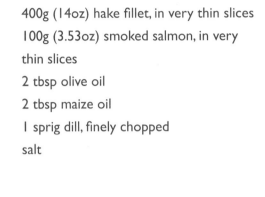

400g (14oz) hake fillet, in very thin slices

100g (3.53oz) smoked salmon, in very

thin slices

2 tbsp olive oil

2 tbsp maize oil

1 sprig dill, finely chopped

salt

1   Lay the hake fillets on plastic foil and then press slightly flat.

2   Divide the salmon over the fillets and sprinkle lightly with salt.

3   Roll them up tightly and place in the fridge for 2 hours.

4   Cut the roll into very thin slices and portion them onto 4 plates.

5   Brush with olive oil and put them under the grill for ½ a minute.

6   Garnish with a sprig of dill.

FILLED ROLLED BEEF

1kg (35.3oz) beef (ask the butcher to cut
a thin piece)
salt and pepper

For the filling
1 tbsp olive oil
1 onion, diced
4 cloves garlic, cut into small pieces
2 tbsp dried tomato, finely chopped
pinch of basil
pinch of thyme, just the leaves
1 sprig rosemary, finely chopped

1   Preheat the oven to 220 °Celsius (425°Fahrenheit), gas mark 7.
2   Heat the oil in the pan and fry the onion and the garlic for a little
    while, stir in the tomato and herbs and then take all the ingredients
    out of the pan.
3   Sprinkle the meat with salt and pepper; spread the filling on the
    meat and roll up and tie with kitchen string.
4   Put the meat in a roasting tin and cook for 10 minutes at 220°C
    (425°Fahrenheit), gas mark 7 and then another 20 minutes at
    180°Celsius (356 Fahrenheit °) gas mark 4-5 till it is ready.
5   Take the rolled beef out of the oven and let it rest for 10 minutes
    before serving.

WHITE CHOCOLATE MOUSSE

WITH PASSION FRUIT AND CHOCOLATE CAKES

2 egg whites

150ml (5floz) cooking cream

500g (17.6oz) white chocolate

500ml (16.9floz) cream, whisked until slightly stiff

flesh of 4 passion fruit

Ingredients for the cakes

1 egg

25g (0.88oz) sugar

25g (0.88oz) flour

100g (3.53oz) white chocolate, grated

75ml (2.54floz) whipping cream, slightly stiff

70g (2.5oz) cream cheese

1   To make the chocolate mousse, whisk the egg whites until very stiff. Warm the cooking cream and melt the chocolate into the mixture.

2   Allow the mixture to cool a little and stir in the cream that has been whisked until slightly stiff. Spoon the egg whites carefully into this.

3   Portion the mousse into 4 dessert glasses and put these in the fridge for at least 4 hours to stiffen.

4   To make the cakes, preheat the oven to 180°Celsius (356° Fahrenheit) gas mark 4-5.

5   Whisk the egg with the sugar and then spoon in the flour. Add 25g (0.88oz) of grated chocolate. This can also be melted beforehand.

6   Pour the chocolate mixture into little cake moulds and put these in the oven for 20 minutes.

7   To make the top layer of the cakes, bring the cooking cream to the boil. Melt 75g (2.6oz) of chocolate and stir in the cream cheese.

8   Pour the mixture over the cakes and allow this to stiffen for 2 hours.

9   Take the chocolate mousse glasses from the fridge and divide the passion fruit over them.

10   Serve with a scoop of vanilla ice cream and three small chocolate cakes.

INDEX
FROM A TILL Z